No Holds Barred Fighting:
The Book of
Essential Submissions
Mark Hatmaker

Photography by Doug Werner

TRACKS

Tracks Publishing
San Diego, California

No Holds Barred Fighting:
The Book of Essential Submissions
Mark Hatmaker

Tracks Publishing
140 Brightwood Avenue
Chula Vista, CA 91910
619-476-7125
tracks@cox.net
www.startupsports.com
trackspublishing.com

Copyright © 2009 by Doug Werner
10 9 8 7 6 5 4 3 2 1

Publisher's Cataloging-in-Publication

    Hatmaker, Mark.
      No holds barred fighting : the book of essential
    submissions / Mark Hatmaker ; photography by Doug
    Werner.
      p. cm.
    Includes index.
    LCCN 2009927898
    ISBN-13: 9781884654336
    ISBN-10: 1884654339

      1. Hand-to-hand fighting. 2. Mixed martial arts.
    3. Wrestling. I. Werner, Doug, 1950- II. Title.

GV1111.H336 2009   796.81
                          QBI09-600067

Books by Mark Hatmaker

No Holds Barred Fighting:
The Ultimate Guide to Submission Wrestling

More No Holds Barred Fighting:
Killer Submissions

No Holds Barred Fighting:
Savage Strikes

No Holds Barred Fighting:
Takedowns

No Holds Barred Fighting:
The Clinch

No Holds Barred Fighting:
The Ultimate Guide to Conditioning

No Holds Barred Fighting:
The Kicking Bible

No Holds Barred Fighting:
The Book of Essential Submissions

Boxing Mastery

No Second Chance
A Reality-Based Guide to Self-Defense

Books are available through major bookstores
and booksellers on the Internet.

Dedication
This book is dedicated to the elite MMA athletes of the world. Your accomplishments provide the data that fuels what is between these covers. Thank you for the concrete information and thank you for the entertainment.

Acknowledgements
Phyllis Carter
Kylie Hatmaker
Kory Hays
Jackie Smith
Mitch Thomas
Shane Tucker

Warning label
The fighting arts include contact and can be dangerous. Use proper equipment and train safely. Practice with restraint and respect for your partners. Drill for fun, fitness and to improve skills. Do not fight with the intent to do harm.

Contents

How to use the NHBF manuals

This book and the others in this series are meant to be used in an interlocking synergistic manner where the sum value of the manuals is greater than the individual parts. What we strive to do with each manual is to focus on a specific aspect of the twin sports of NHB/submission wrestling and give thoughtful consideration to the necessary ideas, tactics and strategies pertinent to that focus. We are aware that this piecemeal approach may seem lacking if one consumes only one or two manuals, but we are confident when three or more manuals have been studied, the overall picture or method will reveal itself.

Since the manuals are interlocking, there is no single manual in the series that is meant to be complete. For example, although *NHBF: Savage Strikes* is a thorough compendium on NHB/self-defense striking, it is bolstered with a side-by-side study of *Boxing Mastery*. While the book *NHBF: Killer Submissions* introduces the idea of chaining submissions and can be used as a solitary tool, it is made stronger by an understanding of the material that preceded it in the first submission manual, *NHBF: The Ultimate Guide to Submission Wrestling.*

And so on and so forth with each manual in this series. With that out of the way, let's dive into the world of MMA competition and separate the wheat from the chaff.

Mark Hatmaker

Primer

Everyone seems to be interested in the best or greatest of almost everything. We revel in top ten lists, the best rankings, hierarchies of any and all sorts. The rankings can be something as meaningful as the most influential books in history or as vacuous as VH1's "Cutest Child Stars of All-Time." (I watched that show. I have no idea why. Your pity and disdain are noted and well-deserved.)

We enjoy rankings because human beings are pattern seeking, systemizing animals. Ratings are fun and sometimes useful. There are two ways to rank, and one is, by far, more useful than the other. The two ways to rank, of course, are subjective and objective.

Subjective rankings are merely matters of taste. Is one child star quantifiably cuter than another? How does one actually measure cuteness? Have we developed a calibrated cuteometer that renders such rankings foolproof? Is the Oscar winning film for best picture in a given year actually the best film produced that year? Is 1998's "Shakespeare In Love" really a better film than that same year's "Saving Private Ryan"? My subjective meter says, "Hell no!"

You get the picture. Subjective rankings are entertaining and perhaps of use in finding new music, new film or realizing that Punky Brewster is far cuter than Doogie Howser, but subjective ratings are meaningless by consensus or fiat. I mean that a select individual or individuals declare Coke is better than Pepsi, and so it is. While this is blasphemy to Pepsi drinkers, the declaration is meaningless. Coke drinkers keep drinking Coke, and Pepsi drinkers keep drinking their far inferior beverage. Win-win.

The second way to rank — the objective — is where the money is. Objective rankings presume that there is a definite set of criterion to be measured. The ability to make quantifiable estimations of a subject can lead us to rankings that are qualitative.

Objective rankings do not concern themselves with cute child stars or pizza toppings. Objective rankings leave opinion behind and turn to the laboratory. When I say laboratory, it is any location where objective tests take place.

Sure, some laboratories are complete with white lab coats, beakers and retorts filled with substances beyond my ken. But a laboratory also can be a motor speedway — which car is fastest? The lab says, that one. A lab can be a gym with an Olympic bar and weight plates — who can lift more? He can. A lab can be a hiking trail — who can make it to the top first? She can. When we move beyond opinion to results, we are seeing objective testing at work. Empirical data. The scientific method at play.

This second renaissance of MMA (the first rebirth occurred at the beginning of the last century) has provided us with laboratories all over the world. The Octagons, cages and rings where MMA competition takes place have been entertaining and supply solid, objective results about what does and does not work in

The Octagons, cages and rings where MMA competition takes place have been entertaining and provide us with solid, objective results about what does and does not work in the sport of MMA.

the sport of MMA.

This book is a primer, an elementary manual, of what you need to know about MMA competition. It's not what you need to know because I say it is. It's what you need to know because the objective data says that this is what you need to know. What you must know. What you have to know. In other words, the essentials.

MMA only

I am dealing with results pertaining to one specific arena — the world of Mixed Martial Arts competition. Yes, I know we usually try to dovetail MMA and submission grappling, since the sports are so closely related, but after much thoughtful consideration, I see the relation between the two sports to be a bit more distant than I originally assumed. The twin sports are less siblings and more like cousins twice removed.

The data herein is not to be construed or twisted to accommodate what goes on in the street. To do so is a grave mistake as we've already addressed in the street self-defense volume, *No Second Chance*.

It's not what you need to know because I say it is. It's what you need to know because the objective data says that this is what you need to know.

We must understand that blending striking and grappling forces changes on the way these sports are played in isolation. While boxing is a formidable game in and of itself, it has to be played differently for the MMA arena or you will find yourself on the mat. Muay Thai is without a doubt a devastating striking sport, but you've got to alter your game when it's all in. As for the grappling-only perspective, allow me to paraphrase the late, but great Carlson Gracie, "Punch a Jiu-jitsu black belt in the face once and he becomes a brown belt. Punch him twice and he becomes a purple belt."

One more time, the information within is strictly for MMA competition.

1 My empirical data ate your dogma

I'm going to gamble that you prefer evidence over simple dogma.

If you were going to step inside a cage or a ring, would you rather have advice based on tradition and opinion or advice based on evidence? Be honest as you answer this question. You are putting yourself in harm's way. Everybody gets hit in a fight, even good fighters (they just get hit less).

Do you want hearsay? Do you want strategies and tactics uttered out of habit that don't have much practical thought behind them? Do you want to train or drill ideas that are related to a different environment than the one you are entering? This is your body you are putting on the line. Wouldn't it be wise to arm yourself with the best information available?

I'm going to gamble that you prefer evidence over simple dogma. If at any point in your training, you confront a bit of evidence (not advice) that butts against what you have assumed to be correct, well, that's terrific. You've learned something. Discard the underperforming tool and get to work incorporating the new tool. This acceptance of evidence has nothing to do with personal likes or dislikes, allegiances or alliances, respect or disrespect. It's simply acknowledgment of truth.

Advice usually is offered with good intentions. For the most part, people are well-meaning. But if the advice fails the evidentiary test, then it's gotta go bye-bye. This quote from the late Michael Crichton fuels this perspective, "Intentions are meaningless, all that matters are results."

I bring up the need for nondogmatic thinking because the sport of MMA has had a curious history. Unlike most sports, some branches of MMA have come to us from avenues that allowed the art to become cloaked in a bit of crypto-mysticism or strict codes of unwavering lineage and tradition stopping just short of fealty reminiscent of medieval vassals and lords. This stifles honest questioning and experimentation — the hallmarks of progress.

Other sports operate in a train-drill-practice-scrimmage-play MO. That is, learn what you did right or wrong, incorporate those results into your training and then play again. These sports are using the objective empirical method, whether it is called that or not. We think they are wise to do so. It's not only the scientific method, it's good common sense.

We've all seen films of early ball games or Olympic competitions and marvel at what was and respect the pioneers for their accomplishments. But you notice also that games and individual events have evolved. Johnny Weissmuller and Buster Crabbe swam beautifully in the Olympics of yore, but how do you think they would stack up against Michael Phelps (baked or not)? How would a 1930s era college football team fare against a team today? These are subjective questions, I

Some branches of MMA have come to us from avenues that allowed the art to become cloaked in a bit of crypto-mysticism or strict codes of unwavering lineage and tradition stopping just short of fealty reminiscent of medieval vassals and lords.

know. We can quibble and offer, "Well, if they had access to the same training opportunities and the same resources as we have today" argument … but that proves the point, doesn't it?

They didn't have these resources and opportunities. They were providing the data to foster the astonishing improvements and performances we see today. To paraphrase Isaac Newton, these athletes of yore are the giants upon whose shoulders we stand today.

No sport would hamstring itself with blind obeisance to an outmoded tactic, strategy or tool. When Jim Corbett began dissecting the Great John L. Sullivan with the "new technology" of the jab, traditionalists didn't suppress the jab and insist that we go back to the old way. Boxers the world over took a look at early film of Gentleman Jim and eagerly adopted the jab as their own.

In the 1968 Summer Olympics, Dick Fosbury won the gold medal in the high jump with what is called the

Fosbury Flop. Prior to Fosbury's innovation, athletes had cleared the bar with techniques such as the straddle, the western roll, the eastern cutoff and the scissors jump. Previous high jumpers were landing either on sand or low matting and therefore had to be a bit more careful. The advent of deep foam landing surfaces allowed for a more carefree technique, and Fosbury's Flop evolved to exploit this change. Fosbury's Flop wasn't discounted or ignored. It was quickly adopted and incorporated by other athletes.

We've got to know what wins fights and what gambits get us into trouble. We must quantify offense and defense in a qualitative manner that allows us to build hierarchies of utility.

And that's the way it should be whether in sports, business or everyday life. Always evolve, always adapt, always pay attention. Be willing to slough off what pays low dividends in favor of that which pays high yields.

Let us clarify that high yield goal further. We want high yields based on safe investments. We don't want our training to echo the current economy where projected high yields were based on risky investment tools and ended up paying squat. We want our training to be safe vehicles that still pay high returns. We don't want to be the gamblers with "a system" visiting the Bellagio

Casino in Las Vegas hoping for a bit of Lady Luck based on something we caught in the film, "21."

No, we want to be the Bellagio itself with house odds at all times. You want to be the Bellagio that offers a game that will win more often than not. As soon as casino customers start pulling more than you do on an individual game, then that game either has to be tweaked or it's gotta go. Casinos stay solvent over the long haul, gamblers don't. Be the Bellagio.

In our goal to be the Bellagio, we've got to know what wins fights and what gambits get us into trouble. We must quantify offense and defense in a qualitative manner that allows us to build hierarchies of utility. We have to recognize what might be "Black Jack" in one version of combat sports might be "bust" in MMA. To shed this casino metaphor and move to the concrete, let's look at the Omaplata submission.

The Omaplata (coil lock or leg wrap DWL to wrestlers) is a high percentage submission in Jiu-jitsu competition and submission wrestling tournaments. How does it stack up in MMA? Of the 640 fights examined for this study, the Omaplata was attempted 48 times and finished zero times.

These 640 bouts comprised the best competitors — fantastic Jiu-jitsu players, excellent wrestlers, formidable kick boxers. Athletes who, in all probability, had a better than average working knowledge of how to set up and use this submission that serves so well in other arenas. Yet in MMA, the numbers show it to be an underperforming investment tool.

This sort of information comprises this primer. Like statisticians in other sports inform regarding strategy, tactics and draft picks, it is time we use empirical tools with MMA and allow the results to spur us forward. Our sport will evolve, and with that evolution, we will see innovations a la Dick Fosbury and Jim Corbett that will give us new strategies and tactics to factor into our equations. Until then, we need to ensure that the equations we are working with now are accurate.

2 Maddening method

For those who may be curious how I quantified the material in this primer (and it is wise to question any and all sources), I offer the following as an explicatory justification for the conclusions herein.

I focus on the concrete. A fight must have a definite end, either via KO or tap-out.

We surveyed 640 fights. These fights were culled from the last 40 Ultimate Fighting Championship (UFC) events and the last 40 Pride Fighting Championship (PFC) events from the most recent at the time of this writing and then backward chronologically.

I did not start with either the inception of the events or delve into the earliest matches. I gave greater heft to the most recent events for the following reasons.

1. The earlier events used different rule sets than we see now (sometimes drastically different).

2. The early events suffered from the usual growing pains seen in any gestating enterprise — wildly disparate skill levels, less than optimum matchmaking and, in some cases, unusual organization of the event itself that might taint results.

3. More recent events present better matchmaking, higher athletic and technical ability overall, and more

experienced competitors on which to base our results — results that are more pertinent to today's competitor.

What is between these covers is the meat of careful analysis, and you may find some of it surprising, indeed.

I chose the UFC because it is arguably the premier event inside a cage, and the PFC because it holds the same cachet for MMA inside a ring. I wanted to examine the best athletes in the sport in different environments to see how the game must be played as dictated by cage or ropes. I mean beyond the obvious innovations seen in cage drives, cage pins, and the like.

No decisions are factored into any of the results found in this primer. Decisions can sometimes be maddeningly subjective (such as the legendary Vegas decision), so I focus on the concrete. A fight must have a definite end, either via KO or tap-out. Ignoring decisions does not in anyway imply disrespect. It simply is not a selected metric for this particular study.

I didn't include doctor stoppages. Yes, doing such damage to an opponent that a doctor must stop the fight is without a doubt worthy of study, but I wanted to quantify specifically what makes an individual stop either of his own volition or via KO. There are far too many doctor stoppages witnessed in which the doctor is wise to stop the fight for the safety of the fighter, but we detect no decrease in willingness to compete from the stopped fighter. Aiming for doctor stoppages and decisions in your game plan is leaving too much to chance. Again, we will focus only on what is a definite stop via KO or tap-out.

Damage Points. Here's where an unfortunate bit of potential subjectivism leaks into the system. There are times when a fight seems to be won by a single punch, but we all know it was the liver kick 30 seconds prior that did the damage, and everything that followed was merely icing on a slow KO. I tried to confine the results to the eyewitness finishes of each fight and to ignore damage points unless it was absolutely clear that the damage point was what inevitably led to the victory. The following scenario illustrates the quandary.

Fighter A lands a devastating overhand that drops Fighter B. Fighter A follows Fighter B to the mat and rains down a series of quick hammer fists that are defended rather weakly (sounds like many Chuck Liddell finishes, doesn't it?). Eight hammer blows land before the fight is stopped. Here's the dilemma: Do we award the victory to the overhand or to the ground and pound?

Damage points are the only area where I made the occasional subjective evaluation, but I have done my best to assign the win to whatever seems to be the obvious deciding factor. Any mistakes in these subjective evaluations are, of course, mine and I offer my apologies if any of them are awry.

So now you have the method to the primer. It's as

straightforward as I could manage without duplicating my blow-by-blow shorthand analysis that are my notes (trust me, no one needs exposure to the tedious conglomerate of my chicken scratching). What is between these covers is the meat of careful analysis, and you may find some of it surprising, indeed.

3 Pareto's Principle revisited

> In a nutshell, he observed that a minority of causes or events led to a majority of the outcomes. Conversely, a majority of causes or events led to a minority of outcomes.
>
> Huh?

In volume three of this continuing saga on martial study, *NHBF: Savage Strikes,* I introduced the Pareto Principle and how it applies to combat training. At the risk of flogging long-dead horses, the Pareto Principle deserves a second look as the material found in the next section, The Hierarchy of Utility, is tailor-made for Pareto treatment.

For the uninitiated, Vilfredo Pareto was an Italian economist who made a rather useful observation in 1897. In a nutshell, he observed that a minority of causes or events led to a majority of the outcomes. Conversely, a majority of causes or events led to a minority of outcomes. Huh? Let's rephrase Pareto, as is commonly done, and simplify his observation to the 80/20 Rule.

The 80/20 Rule states that 20 percent of the input is responsible for 80 percent of the results. Conversely, 80 percent of the input is responsible for only 20 percent of the results. In case you still haven't wrapped your

> I made the assertion that a small percentage of offensive tools (20 percent) would account for 80 percent of your success.

head around it (it took me a while), let's picture your place of work your fellow employees.

Pareto's Principle or the 80/20 Rule states that out of 10 employees, 2 do the majority of the real work (80 percent). The remaining 8 employees surf the net, chat with one another, text most the day away and, as a result, contribute only about 20 percent of the overall work. I'll wager that this example immediately rings true for your own place of employment, and that you can name those who are 20 percenters (the go-getters) and those who are the dead weight.

In a completely fair work environment (no such thing) those 8 folks would get canned and one more 20 percenter added to take up the slack. The 80/20 Rule applies across the board to most endeavors that allow for cost-to-benefit analysis — investments, work, projects, even relationships. But here we are concerned about how it applies to combat sports training.

In *NHBF: Savage Strikes*, I made the assertion that a small percentage of offensive tools (20 percent) would account for 80 percent of your success. With that in mind, I then urged the reader to make an assessment of all the offensive tools and determine which delivered the highest returns. Once this inventory was made, I stated that these tools should receive approximately 80 percent of your training attention since they will provide the most bang for the buck. Tools evaluated as low return on your investment (20 percent or less) should have less time (in some cases zero time) dedicated to their practice. I still stand by these assertions, but what I failed to present at the time was a bona fide way to evaluate and distinguish the 20 percenters from the 80 percenters. That's where this book comes into play — it's about Pareto's Principle and building a Hierarchy of Utility. More on that in the next chapter.

Now let's illustrate Pareto's Principle in action in our particular area of concern. Let's assume we want to build a striking base. We need to determine how much time to spend training boxing and how much time to spend honing our Muay Thai skills. Do we devote ourselves to each discipline equally? Both are undeniably devastating striking schemata within their own rule sets. But does one hold more utility to the Mixed Martial Artist than the other?

We studied 640 fights. How many victories were the result of boxing (pure punching technique)? The answer is 96. How about victories via Muay Thai kick? The answer is 14.

A ratio of 96 to 14 is easy to grasp. Does one mode of attack seem to present itself as more useful in top level competition than the other? The numbers say yes. To examine this in greater detail, 12 of those 14 victories came via head kick. This information is important because it shows that a head kick definitely has a place in the hierarchy. We can see where that ranking might be when we compare 96 to 14 on return investment. Are these numbers all we need to know to schedule our MMA striking training? Not quite.

Another important set of numbers is 12 out of 640 fights. No, 12 is not the number of victories via head kick repeated. This 12 is the number of slips following an attempted head kick. In other words, for every victory via head kick, an elite athlete lost his balance or slipped to the mat as the result of launching his own offense. Twelve times an offensive gambit was launched that placed the athlete in trouble through no effort from an opponent. This compares to NASA and the space shuttle. For every successful shuttle mission, there are an equal number of flash fires on the launching pad. Those are 50/50 odds for success or failure and, perhaps, an argument for grounding the shuttle.

Zero. That's the number of slips occurring from any other offensive gambit. Launching punches or knees resulted in zero slips. Zero versus 12 head kicks that led to instances of self-jeopardy.

Now, let's look at all of these numbers again and see what they tell us.

640 fights
96 victories via straight boxing
12 victories via head kick
12 slips to the mat placing oneself in a defensive position via head kick
0 slips via other offense

A strict interpretation of Pareto's Principle dictates that we observe this hierarchy and budget more training time toward the high return offense (boxing) and tweak down the time we spend firing head kicks in both training and in competition. This numbers game is what this primer is about — combining Pareto's Principle with a quantifiable Hierarchy of Utility while discarding dogmatic assumptions.

Part of that evolution, I am certain, will be better analysis and careful use of fight metrics.

The athletes who take this sport into the future will be using whatever advantage they can muster to make a positive evolution possible. And part of that evolution, I am certain, will be better analysis and careful use of fight metrics.

4 Hierarchy of Utility

The Hierarchy of Utility strips away personal preferences and ranks offensive tactics and strategies in descending order of success. In other words, those tools that account for the highest number of victories are located at the top of the hierarchy, and those with the lowest are at the bottom.

> Those tools that account for the highest number of victories are located at the top of the hierarchy, and those with the lowest are at the bottom.

A pragmatic training regimen ideally gives the greatest weight toward training the tools at the top of the hierarchy and less attention to those at the bottom. By taking the casino route as opposed to the gambler's, we can cultivate a far more successful and scientific game plan as opposed to one composed of tradition or chance.

Please do not mistake my urging of adherence to the highest percentage tools as an argument for giving up on experimentation or innovation. On the contrary, use the Hierarchy of Utility to school the fundamentals, to seat deeply the must-knows and then (and only then) allow your innovation to branch from probabilities.
The Hierarchy of Utility will contain few surprises to longtime participants or followers of MMA. The hierarchy follows the standard principle of success we see

in most endeavors — Keep It Simple Stupid (KISS). KISS is another rephrasing of Pareto's Principle. KISS reflects the fact that, more often than not, a handful of fundamentals are responsible for the majority of the results.

With Pareto and KISS in mind, much of what is found within these pages is not new information in the technique/vocabulary sense, but rather it is the application, the setups, the concrete positioning in the Hierarchy of Utility that gives new and significant heft to older information. Since the fundamentals are key, we will be scrupulous about delineating them.

As we trace the Hierarchy of Utility, we will offer proper form, clean technique, essentials of setups and variations of attack. It is often the small changes in technique calibration that account for success or failure. Consider it in terms of the art/science of orienteering in any Adventure Trek/Eco-Challenge type of event. The smallest incremental deviation (even of inches) when charting your trail can account for a miss by a mile or more in the end. We must treat the fundamentals, the "boring" standbys (the jab, the ride, the rear-naked choke and the like) with utmost care and attention. The Adventure Trekker knows that the hiking, the white-water kayaking, the cliff traverse are the meat and glory of the event, but he also knows that if he screws up the compass work in the beginning, it's all for naught.

The Hierarchy of Utility is your compass. And due diligence paid to the top of the list will get you where you want to go.

5 Hierarchy of Futility

If we invert the Hierarchy of Utility, we get a bizzaro world view of what we may want to spend far less time cultivating (or if we want to spend any time on these low return investments). The items at the bottom of the hierarchy are included because they did account for a victory or two, thus proving their efficacy in some sense of the word. But we should look at their positional rankings and schedule training time accordingly.

If you do not see a specific finish listed in the Hierarchy of Utility, whether it be a jump-spinning crescent kick or a flying arm bar, that's for one of two reasons:

1. The technique was never attempted in any of the 640 fights surveyed.

2. Any attempts by the technique did not result in a single victory.

We look at the evidence of absence on the hierarchy and determine, in all likelihood, a technique does not appear because it was never utilized. (I never did see that jump-spinning crescent kick.) From this absence we can surmise one of two things.

1. Elite athletes hold the absent technique in such low regard in terms of effectiveness that they choose to exclude it from their offensive vocabulary.

2. The elite athletes are somehow ignorant and missing

the boat by foolishly disregarding a bona fide winner.

You choose which of the two explanations you think best suits the facts. I think that the elite athletes probably have chosen wisely in regard to their profession.

In some cases an offensive tool is not on the hierarchy, but not for lack of trying. This survey saw many instances of attempts of various techniques that don't appear on the hierarchy because they simply did not garner a single win in any of the sampled fights.

If an offensive tool is at the bottom of the hierarchy, you are looking at a low return on your investment.

One case in point is the Omaplata (coil lock). Despite 48 attempts with this tool, which has proven so effective in submission-only environments, and despite all of the exuberant cheering when we see this technique being set up, it finished the fight zero times. (A musing on why this might be the case appears in the next section).

So if it's at the bottom of the hierarchy, you are looking at a low return on your investment. If it does not appear in the hierarchy at all, well, then you might be looking at elite fighters missing the boat on a potentially formidable tool, or a successful tool in one arena that translates poorly to the MMA environment.

There is one other possibility ...

Caveats regarding
the Hierarchy of Futility

So far we have two reasons for a poor showing or lack of showing in the hierarchy. The first is ignorance of the tool in question. A tool might actually be effective, but the current incarnation of the sport does not support its appearance in the event. Ignorance, we must clarify, can be ignorance of the tool itself or, reason number two, ignorance in effectively setting up the tool.

We can imagine that there may be some offensive tools floating around out there that haven't broken the barrier yet.

Ignorance of a tool does not preclude its effectiveness. Prior to the jab showing up in boxing in the late 19th century, boxing was doing just fine. But once it was introduced and well understood, it quickly became the mainstay, if not the bread and butter, of the sport. Royce Gracie's victories via rear naked chokes during the 1990s brought another tool to the front of the pragmatic fighter's mind. Before either of these tools appeared, they were not any less effective, but were little-known, undervalued, disregarded or misunderstood.

We can imagine that there may be some offensive tools floating around out there that haven't broken the barrier yet. We need to keep our minds open enough to look at new toys and put them through the stress test in the off chance that it's the new jab. But, at the same time, we must realize that KISS and Pareto's Principle is right more often than not.

As said, ignorance may come in the form of setups as well. That is, we may see the tool attempted (the Omaplata, for example). Perhaps the tool itself is not flawed, but the current mode of setup inhibits success. Again, we must experiment and stress test low percentage tools under various setup conditions to see if an underperforming tool might warrant a place in the hierarchy after all.

If we stay mindful of the two caveats of ignorance, not discount a tool out of hand, stress test the tool or its setups, and in the end discover that it still underperforms, then you have a tool that sucks. Once you've determined suckage of any sort, delete that tool or setup from your system and stay smart by being the Bellagio.

6 Bellagio Hypothesis

A few more words before the Hierarchy of Utility itself and the entertainment portion of the presentation. I'm going to tip my hand and present what is, essentially, my conclusion regarding this research here rather than wait until the end. I consider this observation so integral that you will see it again at the conclusion of this book.

First, I have a confession. I'm a technique junkie. Submission connosouier. Love 'em, love 'em, love 'em. I once heard the great Gene LeBell described as a man who's forgotten more submissions than most people will ever know. I thought that was an estimable goal to shoot for. I may never hit it, but it's fun trying.

I offer the confession so you can better understand what follows. No matter how much I love submissions, I admit that their place in the Hierarchy of Utility is not as well positioned as I would like. I would love to see stunning technical submissions hold precedent, but the truth is they don't. Again, intentions and desires are meaningless. All that matters are results.

Submission junkie that I am, I must content myself with the fact that some submissions do hold sway, some could use fine tuning, and there may be a few lurking in the shadows of ignorance that deserve to see the light of day. But a close study of the Hierarchy of Utility shows that other aspects of the game will provide greater returns statistically despite my "I'd like to see" musings.

Old school

With my submission junkie bubble a bit deflated, I am thankful that another aspect of my overall training philosophy seems on target. We've always adhered to a training continuum that ranks broad aspects and attributes in order of utility. This was an early form of the Hierarchy of Utility.

That old school continuum is:

1. Conditioning
You can know every strike, takedown and submission in the book, but without the horsepower under the hood or the gas in the tank, you have wasted your education.

2. Positioning
Before any punch is thrown, any shot is taken, any submission is set up, there has to be a jockeying for efficient position. Once we have proper position, then we can move on to the next thing.

3. Striking — Vertical or horizontal

And last, and as research would have it, a bit on the least side …

4. Submissions

That old school continuum turns out to be more on the money than I first suspected. The in-depth research conducted for this book allows me to expand on this continuum and offer an enhanced version, which we call The Bellagio Hypothesis.

New school

The Bellagio Hypothesis is an expanded iteration of the old school continuum that focuses on the highest percentage returns on investment from maximum to least.

The Bellagio Hypothesis Continuum is:

1. Conditioning
2. Boxing
3. Shooting
4. Clinch work
5. Parterre
6. Ground and pound
7. Submissions

The Bellagio Hypothesis Continuum is supported time after time by elite level competition. Yes, there are outliers that deviate from this hypothesis (we'll deal with those later), but the hypothesis is named for the Bellagio to reflect its basis on house odds.

Let me expound on the listed elements of the Bellagio Hypothesis.

Conditioning

No victories in this study can be attributed directly to zero gas in the tank or from being overpowered because that's not the rule set. You'll never hear Jimmy Lennon, Jr. say, "The fight stopped at two minutes and thirty-two seconds of the second round with a victory via a better physiological adaptation to high stress anaerobic work!"

Nope, you'll never hear that. But there are many fights

> A tough, tough sport requires tough, tough conditioning. Anything less and everything that follows in the continuum is a waste of your time.

where a renowned and better-schooled fighter gets dragged into the later rounds and is very tired. He'll go flat-footed, begin to mouth breathe, get stuck in lay and pray or clinch leaning scenarios that lead to a loss by an offensive tool that was set up with nothing more than superior conditioning.

With all else being equal (skill level and weight class), competition hinges on who possesses the better conditioning. And as we all know, conditioning in MMA is a grueling mixed bag of attributes. It's not enough to be strong, flexible and possess tremendous aerobic capacity. MMA conditioning is a hardcore combination of all these attributes with the added aspects of power, recovery, speed and mental toughness.

A tough, tough sport requires tough, tough conditioning. Anything less and everything that follows in the continuum is a waste of your time.

Boxing
Initially, what passed for boxing in MMA were caveman swings you see in Toughman competitions. No more. Increasingly we see sharper and sharper boxing skills that do the sweet science proud. Robbie Lawler, Jens Pulvers, or even B.J. Penn's excellent boxing in his

second fight with Sean Sherk, show that actual boxing has found its place in this arena. And it is serving the athletes well.

Of the 640 fights, 81 wins came via punches in bunches (combinations) and 15 via a single punch (always the overhand) bringing us to 96 wins through boxing. But even that does not do justice to boxing's benefits.

The vast majority of recorded finishes in ground and pound were preceded by damaging boxing work. The vast majority of takedowns were set up by boxing (zero takedowns were set up from a kick). Almost every clinch confrontation included boxing as part of the offense. If we add the number of

Boxing is a bread-and-butter tool for today's elite MMA competitors.

victories that came as a result of a flurry of knees and punches thrown together where we can't determine which shot did the trick, we can add another 15 victories.

Boxing is a bread-and-butter tool for today's elite MMA competitors. It would be mind-bogglingly irresponsible to give it short shrift in any MMA training regimen.

Shooting
Shooting or takedown work is maddeningly tough to quantify as we recorded only three takedowns that resulted directly in a KO. On the other hand, we recognize the takedown for what it is — an absolutely vital

Where shooting is the bridge between the vertical and horizontal environments, clinch work is often the roadblock placed upon that bridge.

bridge that gets us from one sport to another.

Without the shot, we have no Mixed Martial Arts, just kickboxing. Sure, kickboxing is great, but that's not our subject. Shooting is the bridge between the vertical and horizontal environments.

While there are a paltry three direct wins recorded from a takedown KO, it goes without saying that possessing keen takedown skills is paramount.

Clinch work

Shooting and clinch work could be placed side by side in the Bellagio Hypothesis. They are almost equal in importance even if zero victories can be racked as a direct consequence of the clinch itself. I think it's safe to say that even casual observers of the sport recognize there is a lot of offensive value occurring here.

Where shooting is the bridge between the vertical and horizontal environments, clinch work is often the roadblock placed upon that bridge. Seldom did this study witness competitors seeking to clinch. The clinch occurs when a competitor foils a takedown attempt. The fight then becomes the clinch.

We must be ever mindful of this hand in glove relationship where the clinch is the product of defended shots. We see many athletes very good at this. Randy Couture will take a shot, if he gets it, that's great. If not, he does not pas de deux within the clinch. He gets to work making the clinch his next offensive tool off the failed shot.

Conversely, fighters like Anderson Silva scrupulously avoid taking a shot themselves. Instead they often turn stuffed shots into clinch affairs where they turn their own defense into an offense. Georges St. Pierre is a textbook example of a fighter who uses both tactics.

Shooting and the clinch are equivalent tools that absolutely must be included in the upper tier of your training schedule.

Parterre

Parterre (sometimes written par terre) is ground wrestling. Parterre has come to mean "on the ground" in the sport of Greco-Roman wrestling, which oddly enough is neither Greek nor Roman in origin, but French. The French dubbed the groundwork of this sport "parterre" after the formalized, intricate gardens that are called parterres. These are gardens with intricate bordered paths and twining walkways bordering meticulously cultivated plants of many varieties. I agree with the French. This analogy of complexity, care and cultivation is apt for the best of what we see in the ground game.

I opt for this term taken from a specific wrestling culture over the more generic "grappling" because parterre implicates the interweaving of species, complexity and refinement that seems to better reflect the hybridized competitors we see today. Seldom do we see top level athletes who are simply wrestlers or just Jiu-jitsu men or fighting within any single discipline. The mix in Mixed Martial Arts seems to be ever more complex, and I predict that we may evolve to a point where the listing of styles in The Tale of the Tape goes the way of dinosaurs, 8-track tapes and Lehman Brothers.

I also use parterre in the Bellagio Hypothesis to distinguish one of the three main aspects of the ground game. We are all familiar, of course, with the importance of ground and pound and submissions. But what is seemingly an even more undervalued bridge than shooting is the simple ability to navigate relatively fluidly while on the ground with no emphasis on striking or submissions.

A careful observation of the competitors in this study reveals that most repeat victors emphasized ground mobility and control (what we have dubbed parterre) over quick rushes to striking or submissions. Essentially they are treating the parterre for exactly what it is — an echo of the original old school continuum's positioning decree.

Parterre recognizes the fact that there is no ground and pound without good riding and good control. Good parterre recognizes that submissions do not exist without pinpoint positioning. Parterre is the unglamorous prerequisite for striking and submissions. Without it the ground game falls into the hands of chance.

Please do not assume that since the chosen word parterre comes from a wrestling discipline that there is any less demonstration of all the word embodies from, say, Jiu-jitsu. Parterre in this hypotheses refers to any and all efficient and effective ground fluidity and control. Parterre strives to assume that evolution-revolution has already taken place, and we have sloughed off the need for "style" labels in our laboratory Tale of the Tape.

What is seemingly an even more undervalued bridge than shooting is the simple ability to navigate fluidly while on the ground with no emphasis on striking or sub-missions.

Ground and pound

The next step in the Bellagio Continuum has been tipped. Parterre leads you to ground striking — yes, before your submissions. Most definitely before. Here's why I make this asser-tion.

Of 640 fights, 114 were finished with ground and pound. By the way, if we add the total wins for striking vertically and horizontally, the striking score is 269.

Of the 640 fights, 187 were finished via submission. You might look at those numbers, 114 ground and pound versus 187 submissions, and deduce that we need to flip these two in the Bellagio Continuum.

But wait a second …

Approximately, 75 percent of the 187 victories via submission were set up with a vicious ground and pound attack that made the acquisition of the submission viable. Many times submission attempts without strikes preceding them were simply ineffective. In a great many cases, the ending submission was in a gray area where the submission was acquired after grave damage via strikes, and it appears that a few more strikes would have done the trick just as easily (in some cases more easily).

If we revise the 75 percent number to a conservative 50 percent of submissions being garnered as a result of effective ground and pound directly preceding them, then add that 50 percent of the 187 submission wins to our already established 114 via ground and pound alone, the ground and pound utility score rises to 207.

If the majority of athletes precede most, if not all, submissions via ground and pound, we would see a significant rise in submission victories.

Actually 207.5 but who wants to halfway win half a fight?

Submissions
We are now at the conclusion of the Bellagio Hypothesis Continuum. Please do not assume that since subs are ranked least in a Hierarchy of Utility, that they do not need work.

They most certainly do.

The Bellagio Hypothesis demonstrates that submission work can be regarded in one of two ways.

1. Submissions are less essential to the game than you might assume (surely less so than I assumed). "Less essential" is a relative term. Organs such as your brain and heart are essential organs since we have only one of each. We all have two kidneys and two lungs and could conceivably live productive lives, as some people do, with only one. But I'm wagering you would rather hold on to your "less essentials."

2. The vast majority of submissions in MMA might be better served by intelligent striking setups as opposed to grappling setups. This study supports the idea that if the majority of athletes precede most, if not all, submissions via ground and pound, we would see a significant rise in submission victories.

Bellagio redux
One more time (I'm lying, I'm sure I'll mention this several more times) a careful reading of the research shows that if we budget our training time according to Pareto's Principle, use the Hierarchy of Utility for menu selection, and then assemble our training thrust according to the continuum suggested by the Bellagio Hypothesis, I am confident that we will see a leaner, meaner MMA athlete. An athlete fueled by observable, demonstrable information provided by the top competitors in the sport today.

OK, enough yakking, lace up the gloves, put in the mouthpieces and let's go to work.

7 Conditioning Gut Checks

We know that conditioning is foremost in the Bellagio Hypothesis. So much so that without commensurate dedication to MMA conditioning, it is safe to predict that all the MMA drill work in the world will be for nada. We've labored that point again and again (even at book length in *NHBF: The Ultimate Guide to Conditioning*) so we don't want to get bogged down in that topic again.

But when something is a vital portion of the game, well, then it's a vital portion of the game and not to be ignored. We provide five Conditioning Gut Checks in this section. These are not workout regimens or routines to be hit daily. For that sort of information, I refer you to the aforementioned conditioning volume in this series.

The Conditioning Gut Checks are challenges devised to test your fitness in various modes of high stress activity. These are the Gut Checks we use for any fighter who says, "I'm ready to fight." Once we hear that pronouncement, even before we check the skill-set, we use the Conditioning Gut Checks to see if the grunt work of the most fundamental aspect of the fighter's game is in line with the desire to fight.

The five Conditioning Gut Checks included in this book are from our roster of 175. If you are curious as to where you stand in your own conditioning, give them a shot. If you don't feel up to them, no sweat. Skip to the technique drills, but never forget that conditioning is job one.

Today's MMA fighter requires such a hard-core level of conditioning across a wide range of stresses that no single Gut Check is sufficient. The five included here are meant to be hit over the course of five days: Gut Check #1 on Day 1, Gut Check #2 on Day 2 and so on.

Ideally, you should pass all five with flying colors. Four out of five is also a respectable score. Three or less means you have some work to do. Failing to meet the standards of the Gut Checks does not necessarily mean that you aren't ready. It means that you may have a little thinking to do about the fact of the pre-eminence of conditioning to MMA.

Gut Check #1

Clean and jerk 30 repetitions in under 5 minutes

Use the following poundages:
Body Weight of 121-140 Pounds — 115 Pounds on the Bar
Body Weight of 141-160 Pounds — 125 Pounds on the Bar
Body Weight of 161-180 Pounds — 135 Pounds on the Bar
Body Weight of 181-200 Pounds — 145 Pounds on the Bar
Body Weight of 201-220 Pounds — 155 Pounds on the Bar
Body Weight of 221-240 Pounds — 165 Pounds on the Bar
Body Weight of 241-266 Pounds — 175 Pounds on the Bar

Rules
● The weight must touch the floor at the bottom of each repetition.
● The weight must be held aloft for one full second at the top of each repetition.
● You must complete the Gut Check in 5 minutes on the nose or less to pass.
● All Gut Checks are pass/fail.

Gut Check #2

Run 5K in 25 minutes or less

This one is a snap for most. With some heavier weight classes it may sometimes push the clock, but the ability to deliver sustained effort over a period equal to five rounds is a must.

Rules
- You must come in at 25 minutes on the nose or less.
- Allowances for hills are already factored in (that's what we have in Tennessee). If you are running a flat course, you should be good to go.

Gut Check #3

Dead lift twice your body weight for 10 repetitions in 5 minutes or less

Rules
- Self-explanatory, but just in case, if you weigh 175 pounds, double that to 350 pounds and perform 10 deadlifts at that weight in 5 minutes or less.
- No lifting belts.
- No lifting straps.
- You may chalk your hands.

Gut Check #4

• 100 squats • 50 push-ups • 25 pull-ups in 5 minutes or less

Rules
- The squats must be full-range of motion. In other words, all the way down and all the way up is a single repetition.
- The push-ups must be full-range of motion — no cheating by simply vibrating in a small range of motion. At the bottom of each push-up, your chin, chest and thighs must touch the mat. At the top, the elbows are locked.

● The pull-ups are (surprise) complete range of motion — arms completely extended at the bottom of the motion. Your upper sternum/breastbone must touch the bar at the top of the motion to insure full range.

Gut Check #5

250 cone hops in 5 minutes or less

Rules
● A jump right and left is one single repetition, not two.
● Jump over the cone, not in front of, or behind the cone.
● The cone (or improvised barrier) must be 18 inches high.

Again, if you pass at least four out of five of the Conditioning Gut Checks, you have a good indicator that your fitness foundation has been attended to. If you passed only three or less, utilize Pareto's Principle and budget your training time accordingly.

8 Strikes

Punches in bunches

Boxing combinations resulted in 81 wins out of 640 fights. The combinations were thrown in multiples of three or more punches, the jab setting up the final onslaught.

We will not go into detailed explanation regarding each individual punch as we have done that at book length in *Boxing Mastery*. What we will provide are several high percentage boxing combinations that deserve hours and hours of your training time.

The following are three-point combos.

● Jab / cross / lead hook

● Jab / cross / lead uppercut

● Jab / cross / rear hook

● Cross / lead hook / cross

● Lead hook / cross / lead hook

● Lead hook / lead uppercut / cross

● Lead hook / lead uppercut / rear hook

● Lead hook body / lead hook / rear uppercut

● Jab / cross body / lead hook

● Jab / rear uppercut / lead hook

● Jab / lead hook / cross

● Jab / lead hook / rear uppercut

● Jab / lead hook body / lead hook

● Jab / lead uppercut / rear hook

● Lead uppercut / rear hook / lead hook

The overhand

Sunday punch

Staying with our boxing supremacy theme, the over-hand is the Sunday punch in MMA. The overhand contributed 15 total wins in one punch KO fashion in this study. Compare that to 12 head kick KOs. Factor zero slippage and the ability to shift gears rapidly from simply throwing an overhand to the remainder of the boxing repertoire, and you may have an argument to cut head kick training time and add it to developing overhand power.

Throwing the overhand

● This punch is delivered with the rear hand in a looping downward arc.

● Think of holding a softball in your rear fist, and you have been challenged to throw the ball to the earth's core in a looping overhand pitch.

Boxing and knees

Boxing and knees thrown in conjunction with one another added 15 more wins to the striking column. The knees used in combination with punches were thrown without benefit of the clinch. Since we have already introduced knee technique in detail in *NHBF: Savage Strikes*, here we will provide a few high percentage boxing/knee combinations.

● Jab / rear knee

● Jab / cross / lead skip knee (below)

● Jab / cross / lead hook / rear knee

● Jab / cross / rear knee /
lead hook / rear knee

● Jab / cross / lead skip knee /
rear knee / cross / lead hook

Knees

Knee strikes alone contributed 14 more victories — 10 via knees inside the clinch and 4 from the always dramatic flying knee. (On the subject of flying — the Superman punch contributed zero wins.)

Despite the repertoire of knees available inside the clinch (point knees, round knees, etc.), the standard clinch up knee is the sole contributor to victory. With the Bellagio Hypothesis and Pareto's Principle in mind, slap on your head clinch and get to work throwing multiple rounds of the clinch up knee.

Good

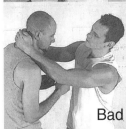

Bad

Head clinch
● Place the palm of one hand on the back of your opponent's head. Not his neck — there's greater leverage at the head.
● Stack your other palm on top of your first hand.
● Squeeze your elbows together and jerk your opponent downward.

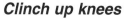

Clinch up knees

● As you jerk your opponent down, surge your rear knee (the knee furthest from your opponent) up and into his face/head.
● Strike with the point of the knee, not the top.
● Plant the striking leg onto the mat and skip the leg that was formerly forward to the rear and strike with the newly positioned rear leg.
● Rinse, wash, repeat.

Flying knee

● To utilize this dramatic tool, take a running start at your opponent and leap into the air jumping off your lead foot.

● Drive the point of the rear knee into your opponent's face.

● As fun as this is, don't lose sight of the fact that it has only four total wins out of 640 fights.

Kicking

 We've addressed kicking in depth in a previous book in this series, *NHBF: The Kicking Bible,* where we presented our hypothesis that the low kick is your primary kicking weapon. The low kick has presented only two wins in the victory column, but it does pay off in spades when one factors in the wearying damage it inflicts.

There were 17 total wins via kick. Ten with a rear kick to the head, 2 with a switch kick to the head, 2 rear kicks to the body, 2 rear kicks to the leg, and one outlier (outliers defined as apparent anomalies) — the spinning back kick to the body courtesy of David Loiseau.

None of the kick victories were fired as part of a combination. They all were launched as solo tools and literally caught the opponent with his hands down. With that in mind, we will forgo combination work here (see *NHBF: The Kicking Bible* for extensive combination work) and simply review the winning kicks minus the outlier.

Rear kick

● Step the lead foot forward 45 degrees and to the outside.
● Pivoting on the ball of the lead foot, lead with your rear hip.
● Fire your rear leg as one solid blunt object into your target.
● The striking surface is the triangular facing surface of the tibia, not the ankle or instep.
● The rear kick can be delivered to the leg, body or head.

Switch kick

● The actual kick mechanics remain the same, all that differs is the manner of getting the lead leg to the rear.

● Execute a quick switch step — jumping the lead foot to the rear and the rear foot forward and 45 degrees to the outside position.

● From this new lead, fire as you would the rear kick.

A special note regarding takedowns

As we've already learned from the Bellagio Hypothesis, the takedown is the bridge between two sports and an absolutely vital portion of the game. We have addressed this subject in *NHBF: Takedowns* and *NHBF: The Clinch,* so we won't labor it again. Suffice to say, although the takedown resulted in only three direct victories via accidental KO upon the initial slam, the takedown precedes every single ground and pound and submission victory. Budget your time accordingly and please do not interpret my glossing over the takedown here as undervaluing an essential tool.

9 Ground and pound

Ground and pound is an immensely useful offensive strategy. The best of the hybrid wrestlers, the cream of the Brazilian Jiu-Jitsu crop, found a major portion of their victories coming from being able to deliver effective strikes from the top position. Notice the word "top." Not a single victory was recorded via striking from the bottom. Seems the old days of up kick knockouts a la Renzo Gracie versus Oleg Taktarov are gone.

A less dramatic correlate to the ground and pound strategy is the ability to ride/control an opponent. No effective ground and pound came from sloppy riding. It all came from athletes who were effective at applying pressure from the top, anticipated movement and rode in front of the movement to maintain top position. The best ground and pounders seemed to think ride, not pin.

Pinning instills a mentality of "I must keep this man right where he is." Pinning requires muscular effort to maintain a static position. Riding, on the other hand, is analogous to the cowboy on the bull in the rodeo. He does not think "Squeeze the bull into a stock-still position with my legs." Such a strategy would be a great waste of energy and time.

Instead, the successful rider anticipates and follows the bull's movements as they hit each herky-jerky permutation. This is arguably a less energy expensive way to go and seems to lead directly to freeing up a limb with which to strike. Ground and pound also preceded the vast majority of successful submission attempts. Using strikes to "soften" an opponent is of paramount value.

Ride drills

With those observations in mind, let's turn to a few drills that educate riding (albeit in a superficial way) and then proceed to fundamental grounding and pounding.

Top Spin

● Have your partner assume a 1/4 position on the mat.
● Using hip and chest pressure, spin to various positions on top of your partner.
● As you do, have him post one hand and then the other to stop your momentum and/or force a change in direction.

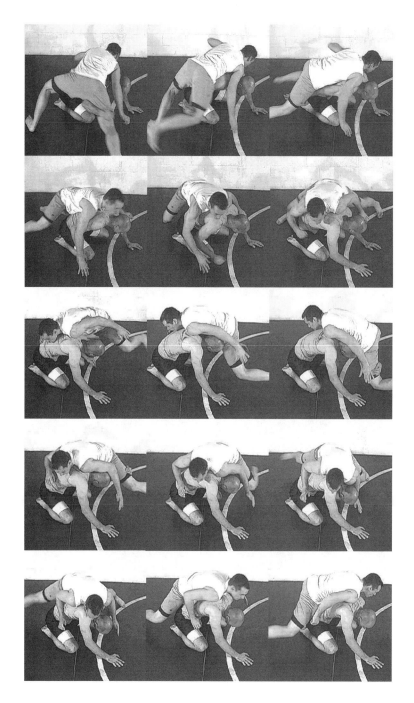

1/2 clock

● Have your partner lie on his back.
● Hit a cross body ride.
● Use chest pressure and travel around his head to a cross body ride on the opposite side.

● Return to the opposite side.
● Your partner can begin to add obstructions and/or bridge and roll escapes from the bottom.
● Note: We stay away from passing over the legs to avoid being stopped in the guard or 1/2 guard.

Spur in

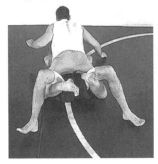

● Hit a top saddle/mount position on your partner.
● Have your partner hit all manner of escapes as you strive to maintain top position with a minimum of lockdown.
● Use hip riding, head pulling and posting to maintain your position.

Knee riding

● Pop your knee onto your partner's chest (not stomach) and extend the free leg for base.
● Have your partner squirm, buck, bridge and roll as you travel from side to side and/or descend into cross body riding or mounting.

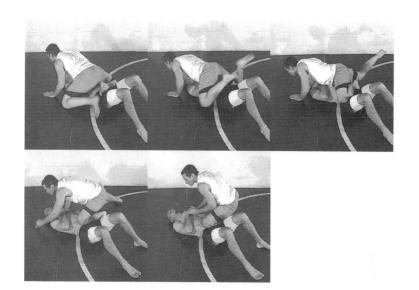

Double knife ride

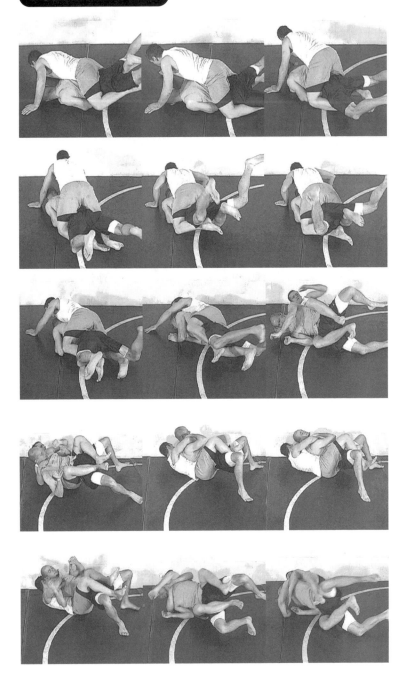

● Place both of your hooks (heels) into your partner's hips from behind.
● Have him roll and attempt to remove them as you ride for long as possible.
● No subs allowed at this point, just ride.

Once you have these rudimentary riding drills down, let's add the pound.

Ground and pound fundamentals
● Gear up — there's very little give for the man with his back to the planet — so play it safe.
● The technique is KISS again. Standard punching (straights and hooks) along with drop elbows and the occasional back elbow (thrown to the side of the head) do the trick just fine.
● Use the following ground and pound Hierarchy of Utility to determine how much time to allot to each position. I'll go ahead and tell you — spend more time striking on the ground than you do seeking submission holds.

Ground and pound Heirarchy of Utility
In descending order of KOs, we see which positions lend themselves to the ground and pound strategy.

1. Inside guard Twenty-eight knockouts came from athletes "trapped" in someone's guard. (A far higher percentage of "trapped" opponents may not have knocked out guard users, but got in a nice share of licks.) It seems wise to take the Fedor Emelianenko route and concern yourself not with passing the guard, but punishing while inside.

Inside guard: Guard clamp
● Head down and elbows sucked tight to hips.
● Fire shots and return to the clamp.

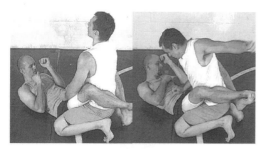

Inside guard: Posture up
● Sit back tall and pick and choose your shots.

Inside guard: Keys
In either case refrain, at all costs, from placing a hand on the mat, or allowing your opponent to sit up. Always post on the man, not the mat (use an elbow on the mat if you must touch it) and throw punches to keep him down.

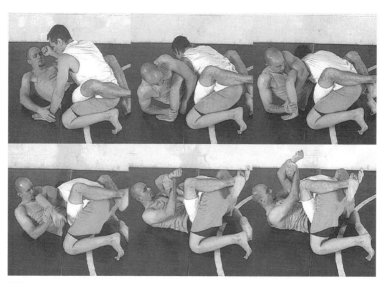

Why you don't post on the mat.

Also, keep in mind to work not just the head. Body shots weary the downed man and, in the case of one fight, can finish — Quinton Jackson over the very tough Igor Vovchanchyn PFC 22. These strategies worked whether closed guard (18), open guard (6) or butterfly guard (4).

2. Mount / top saddle

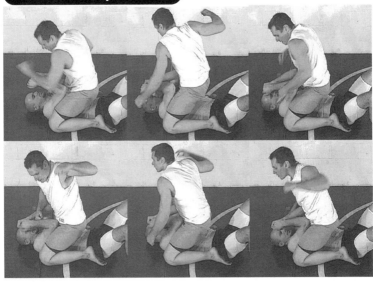

Twenty-six victories via striking from this position. The key is a good ride and picking and choosing your shots. End of story.

3. Cross body

Here the strikes most often came in the form of aggressive hammer fists attacks. Fourteen victories. The standard cross body was used as was the top crucifix.

The top crucifix is illustrated and explained on the next two pages.

Pinning the arm with the shin

Pinning the arm with a figure-4.

Pinning the arm with a scissors.

Top Crucifix

● Pin the near arm with either a shin across the arm or …
● Scissor or figure-4 your legs to trap the arm.

● Underhook the far arm with your hip-side arm.
● Hammer fist or back elbow with your head-side arm.

4. 1/4 position

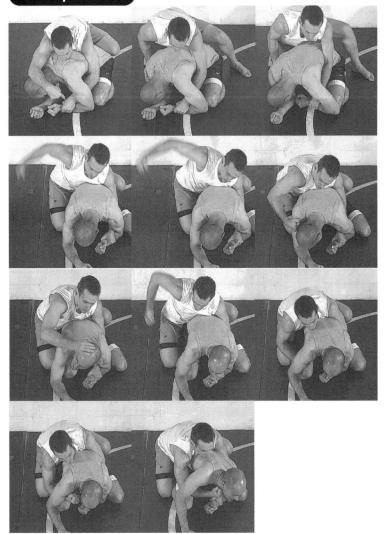

Nine victories from here. There are two ways ...

Far side one-on-one

- Underhook the far arm with your hip-side hand.
- Grip his far wrist with this hand.
- Strike with your free hand.

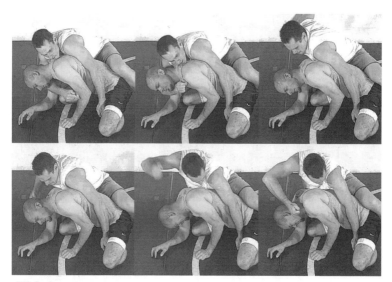

Thigh pry

● Use your hip-side hand to insert into his inner thigh and pry outward using the back of your hand as the contact point on his thigh.

● Seatbelting led to wing rolls and double wrist locks/Kimuras from the bottom man.

5. Back mount

Eight victories came from hooks in/double knife riding — always when the opponent is belly down. Belly up strikes were effective as a softener, but contributed no finishes.

Play with all three versions of the back mount — hooks in (4 victories), no hooks (3) and the single hook (1).

Hooks in

No hooks in

Single hook in

6. Inside 1/2 guard

The Randy Couture school of thought (and a mighty fine school of thought it is) sees the 1/2 guard as an optimistic 1/2 mount. Seven wins came from this approach.

Inside 1/2 guard: Keys

● Keep perpendicular to thwart bottom offense.

● Strive to keep his far arm underhooked to prevent your opponent's escape attempts.

● The better the sprawl the more effective preventative medicine versus full guard attempts.

● Attempt to Turk (lift his leg) with your "trapped" leg.

7. Knee ride

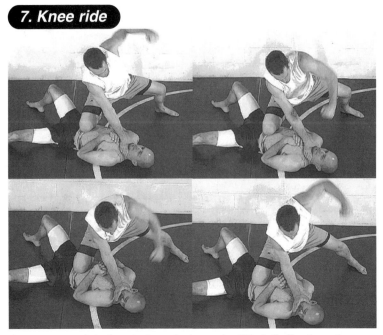

A mere two victories, but a win is a win. Work it. Post on the neck or face.

8. Lateral press / top body hold

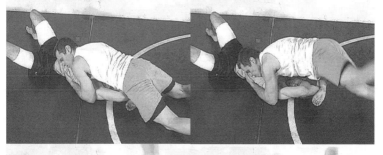

We have one victory via knees
to the head from this position
— obviously from Pride.

9. Grounded

Soccer kick above, stomp left and drop knee below

The remaining ground and pound victories we will classify as grounded. This is the situation where you have your opponent on the ground while you are on your feet.

Again, we still see up kicks, but not to KO effect like in the classic days of Renzo Gracie versus Oleg Taktarov.

Two grounded victories were from the UFC.

Grounded victories from PFC (most of these from Mr. Vanderlai Silva) include six soccer kicks, six stomps and one drop knee.

10 Arm bar

The arm bar is the number one submission in this survey with 54 total wins. But there is a great disparity afoot. Forty of those arm bars came inside the Pride ring, yet only 14 arm bars were successful inside the UFC Octagon.

To be frank, I'm not sure what accounts for this difference in effectiveness. Quality athletes participate in both events, and we see an almost equal number of arm bar attempts, but a big difference in success rates. Let's shelve these anomalous misgivings and move on to successful arm bar technique.

Top saddle / mounted arm bar

The old school pommel horse way did rear its head a couple of times, but these successes were against bone tired opponents. More often than not a tighter approach was called for.

● Underhook your opponent's left arm with your right (at the shoulder).
● Keep your left knee under his right arm and slide it along the mat until the tip of your knee is even with a perpendicular line drawn from the crown of your opponent's head.
● Lean across his body toward his left side while cross facing him with your left forearm.
● Stack your hands underneath his left triceps.
● Step your right calf underneath his left arm.
● Lean toward your right knee as you swing your left leg over his face.
● Cross your feet and drag your hands along his left arm snapping off to transfer to his right arm.
● Pull his arm tight to your chest and arch your hips to the sky to tap.

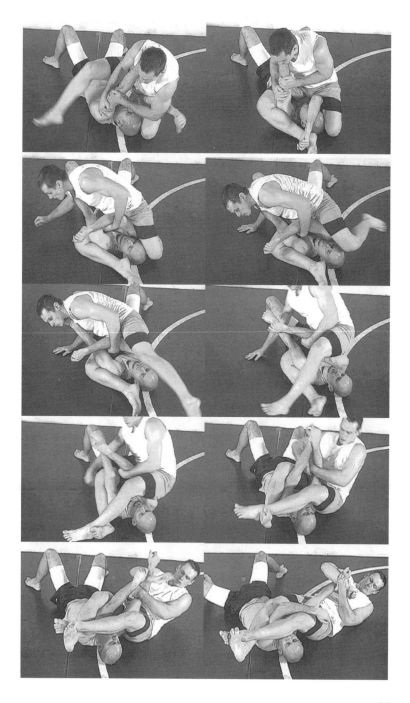

Double cross arm bar from the top saddle / mount

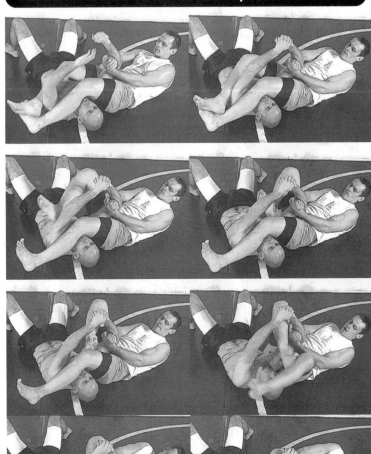

Daniel Gracie used this version to good effect versus Wataru Sakata.

● As you fall back, place the hip-side instep across the near-side of his face.

100

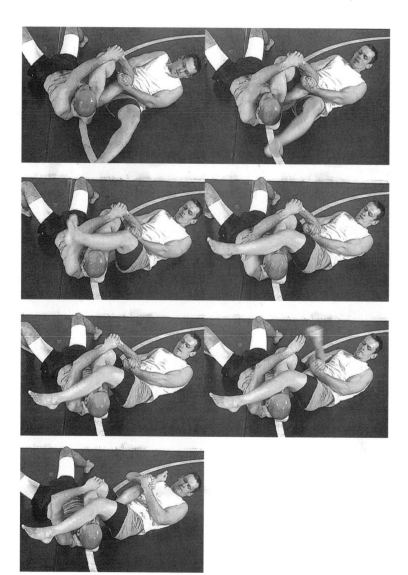

● Cross the other leg over his head in the normal fashion.

Arm bar from squat mount

- Keep your right heel tight to his abs to prevent escape room.
- Slide your left knee even with the top of his head.
- Underhook his right arm with your right.

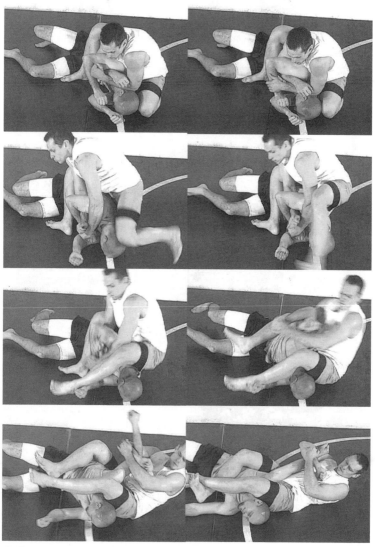

● Post your left elbow on his neck/face.
● Pivot on your elbow and swing your left leg over his head for the arm bar.

Top wrist lock (TWL) / Americana to arm bar

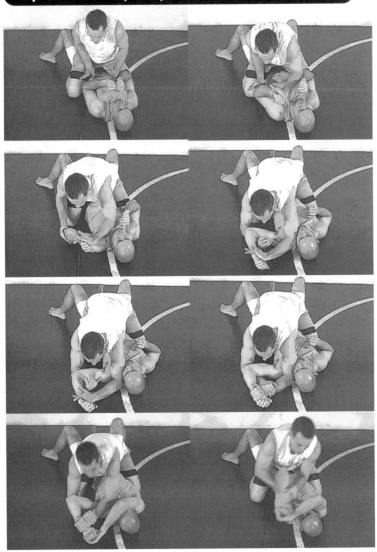

● We saw this nice transition from Gabriel Gonzaga versus Carmelo Marrero.
● Hook a TWL/Americana on his left arm (see Outliers for details).

● Lift his arm and move to a squat mount on his left side.
● Hit your arm bar from here.

Bottom scissors / guard arm bar

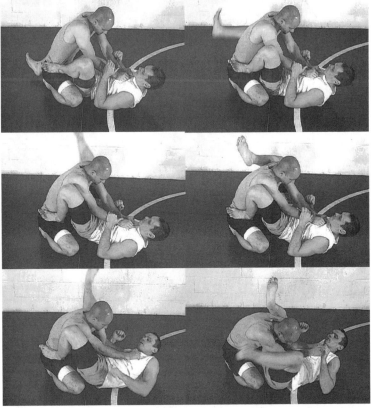

This standard is less about solid setup and more about applying with speed in the midst of chaos (the ground and pound variety of chaos). With that in mind, use the following semi hands-free version as a template to apply the arm bar and drill it under striking pressure because that is the nature of the beast.

● Place the sole of the left foot on your partner's right hip.
● Squeeze tight to his body with your left thigh.
● Ride the right calf high on his back.
● Hit an ab crunch position to create as little drag on the mat as possible.

● Using the hip perch, push with your left foot spinning your body 45 degrees to the right (no less and not away from your opponent).
● Swing the left leg in front of his face.
● Cross your feet.
● Grip his right arm with both hands.
● Arch to tap.

Bottom scissors / guard arm bar with hands

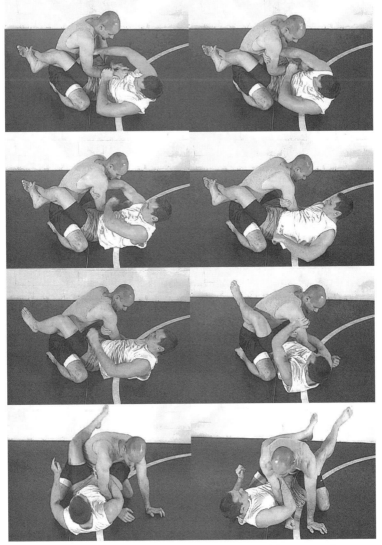

● If the punching is not too heavy, you can add an arm drag against his right arm (use your right arm) before the 45 degree spin.

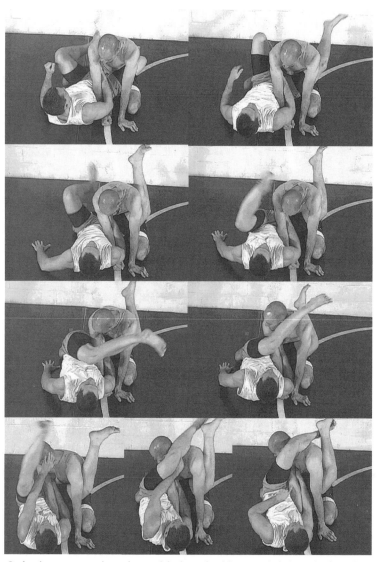

● And you can also shove his head with your left hand after the spin to assist (if you need the help), placing the left leg in front of his face.

Following the arm bar

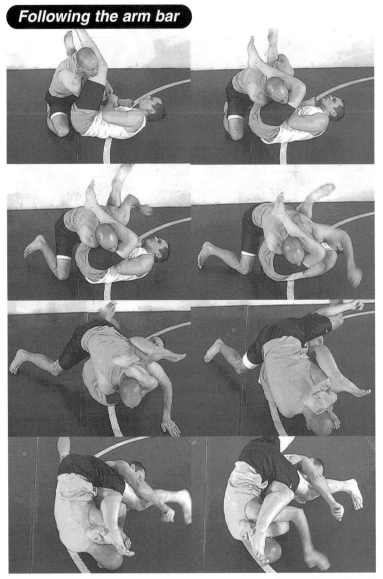

● Drill applying the arm bar from the bottom scissors/guard and leave enough slack for your partner to scramble to different positions.
● Maintain your arm bar and strive to follow whether it goes belly down or belly up and/or transitions to double cross position.

More scrambling, another view

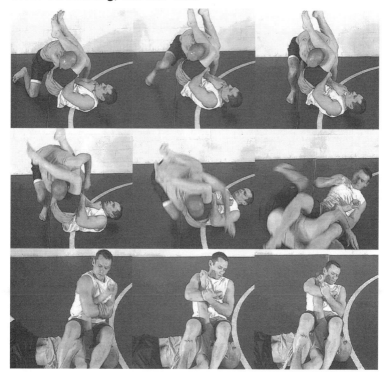

From the 1/4 position

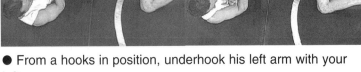

● From a hooks in position, underhook his left arm with your left arm.

● Bring your right leg out of the hooked position and swing it over his head and in front of his face from the left side.

● Grip his arm with both hands and arch your hips through his arm going into a belly down position.

Cross body short arm bar

● This variant isn't as tight due to the single leg control, but it has finished a few (used ably by Matt Hughes in his first encounter with Georges St. Pierre).

● From cross body, underhook your opponent's far arm with your hip-side arm.

● Pull him toward you with this underhook and pop to your feet

in a squat position placing your head-side foot (right foot) on the far side of his head.

● Leaving your feet in place, pivot left 180 degrees and then fall back.

● Your left leg will now be across his face and your right shin should be bracing against his back.

Triangle arm bar

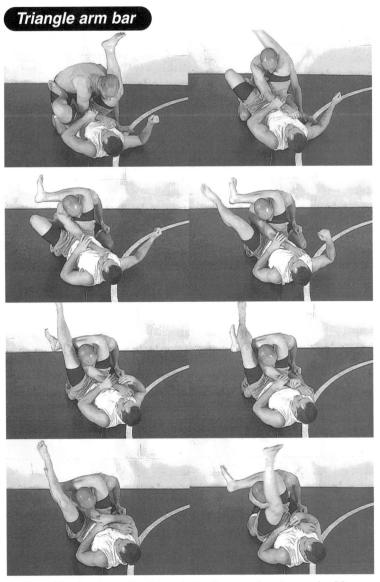

● Transitioning from the triangle to the arm bar is a valuable skill.

● The triangle section will discuss the choke.

● Swing the long tail leg over the face and arm bar the trapped arm.

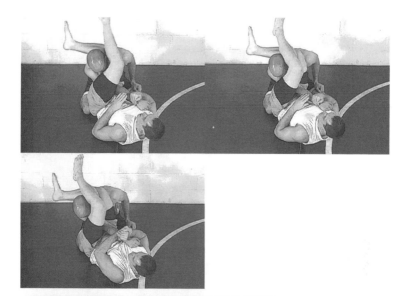

Triangle to double cross arm bar

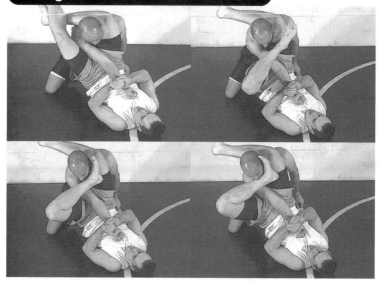

- Used beautifully by Jeremy Horn versus Chael Sonnen.
- From your triangle, cross the long tail shin in front of his face.
- Figure-4 behind the short tail knee.
- Bar the arm already inside.

Hooks in to arm bar

● Start hooks in from the belly up position.
● If you find the choke defense strong, hit the following.
● Underhook his left arm with your left.
● Post your right foot on the mat squeezing his body tight with your knee.

● Use the post to pivot your body 45 degrees to your left.
● Use your right forearm on the left side of his head to drive his head to the right.
● Swing the right leg over his face for the arm bar.

Arm bar following sprawl

Used to good effect by Ben Saunders versus Ryan Thomas.
● You've stuffed the takedown with your sprawl.
● If you are head-to-head and he snags a leg (the left in this case) underhook an arm (here the right) with your left.
● Pivot toward your right and swing your right leg over to put a hook in.

● Figure-4 grip his underhooked arm.
● Jerk him to his side and swing your "trapped" leg over his face for the arm bar.

11 Sleeper

Next in the submission Hierarchy of Utility is the sleeper or the rear naked choke. I prefer the term "sleeper" as the "rear naked choke" nomenclature is borrowed from the gi-work of Judo and Jiu-jitsu, two formidable but distinct combat sports in their own right. "Naked" refers to the nonuse of the gi-sleeve and "rear" gives the impression that the technique can be hit only from behind the opponent. Not so.

So, let's have a look at what reaped 40 victories in elite MMA competition. By the way, we have another disparity here just as we did with the arm bar. Twenty-eight of the sleeper victories were inside the Octagon while only 12 were inside the Pride ring. Again, I can't quite put my finger on why the difference in successes with a similar rate of attempts, but it is worth pondering.

The sleeper

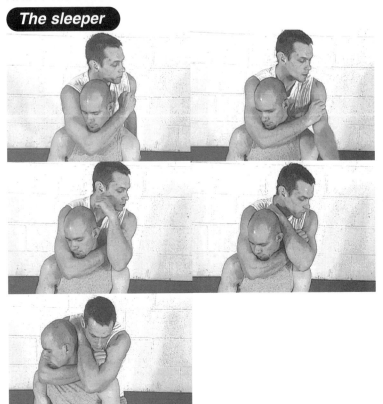

This is the standard.

● The attacking arm encircles the neck with the biceps and forearm on either side of the throat.

● The delicate hyoid bone finds itself "comfortably" notched in the crook of the arm.

● Make a fist with the encircling arm and place it in on the biceps of the free arm.

● Place the fist of the free arm behind your opponent's head.

● Squeeze your elbows together to remove all slack.

● Crunch into your opponent and torque the tightened sleeper toward the bottom elbow/encircling arm (in this case the right).

Follow the sleeper / double hooks

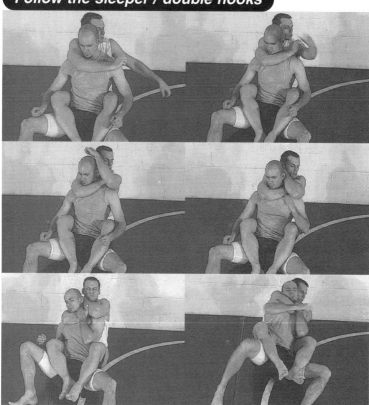

Often once the choke is applied, your opponent will roll through various positions looking for holes through which to escape. You must be able to maintain control no matter what. In the spirit of "no matter what," consider Marcio Cruz's sleeper victory over Keigo Kunihara where he hit both hooks in versus a standing opponent. To aid the "no matter what" goal, try the following drills.

● Place both hooks in.

● Hook up the sleeper and take it to the tap and then back off a comfortable inch or two so your partner has some room to survive.

● Have him move through various positions via rolls, bridging and bucking.

● Your goal is to maintain the integrity of the sleeper and both hooks.

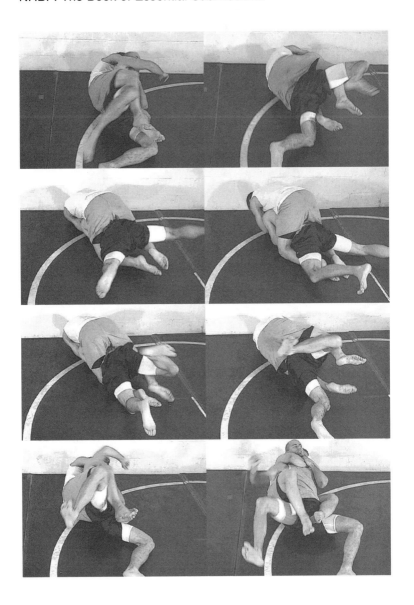

Follow the sleeper / single hook

● Same format as the preceding drill except here you place a single hook.
● Be sure to repeat this drill with the opposite leg hooked as well.

Follow the sleeper / no hooks

A far less common position, but drill it all the same because it has finishing power (Junior Assuncao versus David Lee).
● Hit the comfortable sleeper and zero hooks.
● Go to work.

1-2-3 concept

The preceding drills put the cart before the horse a bit. Yes, we want hooks in when possible, yes we want to hit the sleeper, but there is an oft-missed component that the best players utilize scrupulously. That is the 1-2-3 Concept.

1. You must control the upper body before you throw hooks in or hit the sleeper. This is most often done by underhooking your opponent at one or both armpits and driving his arms away from his body and/or driving him off his base.

2. Once you have control of the upper body, then and only then do you strive to insert hooks. Spur your heels deep into the groin, high along the inner thighs and arch back with your heels to stretch him (the greater the stretch, the easier the sleeper). Do not cross your feet (surprisingly, there is still a lot of that going on).

3. After steps one and two have been taken care of, you can hook the sleeper.

Palm-to-palm choke

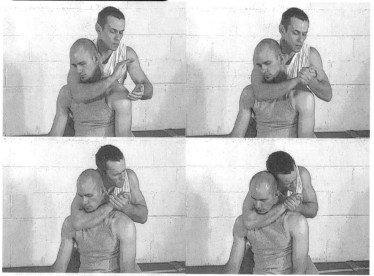

Four of the 12 sleeper victories in Pride actually came in the form of a palm-to-palm choke. Arguably a less "tight" choke, but it apparently works for some.

● The encircling arm is positioned as in the standard sleeper.

● The hands are gripped in palm-to-palm fashion.

● Cinch the grip as tight as possible while cutting the inner wrist bone up and through your opponent's jaw.

Single arm choke

Here we have one variant of the choke that did succeed once
— Dennis Kang versus Amar Suloev. Decide how much you
want to work this one in ratio to the high performers.

● Both hooks in for body control.

● Hook a one-on-one wrist control with one hand (here the left
versus left).

● Hit a single arm choke.

12 Guillotine

What is commonly called the guillotine choke notched a respectable 34 victories. We see a slight tilt toward Octagon success with this technique (16 UFC versus 7 PFC for strict guillotines). The arm included in the guillotine foiled many an attempt, although some were able to finish from here. We'll explore that in a moment.

Guillotine grip

We'll skip the leg work so we can focus on the grip.

● Overhook and encircle your opponent's head.
● Bar grip your encircling hand/wrist with your free hand.
● Pull you hands as high toward your chin as you can manage (for lifting enthusiasts, think upright row).
● Once you have lifted as high as you can, keep your grip high and torque toward your encircling elbow (here the right).

Bottom scissors / guard guillotine

This is the most common position where we see the guillotine succeed. This is primarily because we can add the legs to stretch his body from his head.

● Hook the guillotine grip.

● Add the bonus of stretching him away from your body with your legs.

Bottom scissors / guard guillotine, arm included

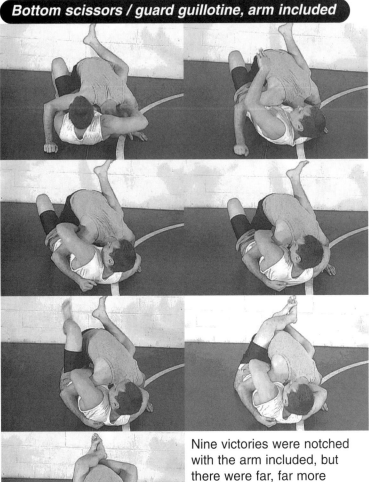

Nine victories were notched with the arm included, but there were far, far more attempts. Don't read that wrong. I think rather than toss the arm-included guillotine, we should emulate what is done correctly. It is a simple matter of overemphasizing the last portion of the standard guillotine grip. ● Hit your guillotine grip.

● Use the legs to stretch away.

● The arm included allows him a bit more "head room" to survive, but emphasizing the torque toward the encircling elbow takes much of that slack out by dint of the elevated wrist grip.

Standing guillotine

There were two standing guillotine finishes in the Pride ring and zero in the Octagon. My guess is that this guillotine is a given in some cases versus a takedown shot. The drive to the fence is permissibly more aggressive and usually leads to a ground version of the move in the cage. Ropes don't call for such line-drive shots, giving greater weight to a standing attempt in Pride.

● From the standing position, hit the guillotine grip.
● It's less about the lift and more about the torque to the encircling elbow.

13 Triangle choke

The triangle choke is a formidable weapon with a surprisingly low rate of return on investment when compared with the number of attempts. I believe the better educated a fighter gets, the less opportunity there is to hit this one. Triangles require tight positioning and equally matched opponents often deny the offensive fighter the optimum position for it to work. Still, we saw 18 total wins out of multiple attempts with 10 inside the Octagon and 8 in the Ring.

Triangle fundamentals

We refer to the leg that tucks behind the knee of the retaining leg as the short tail and the retaining leg as the long tail.

The "triangle" in triangle choke refers to the three constricting surfaces of the choke.
1. The opponent's own trapped arm across the throat.
2. The inner thigh of the short tail leg.
3. The calf of the short tail leg.

If you encounter difficulty in finishing the triangle once it is set, examine your three constricting surfaces and clamp down on any perceived slack.

Open setup drill

There are several schools of thought on beautiful, canny setups. What we saw in high level competition was a mirror of what we encountered with the arm bar — quick initiation snapping the triangle on with little to zero actual setup. Let's turn to a speed drill to help educate this "open setup" method.

● Have your partner feed his left arm between your legs.
● Place your left foot on his hip.
● Post on this foot and elevate high and hard — essentially hitting him with your cup (sorry about that).

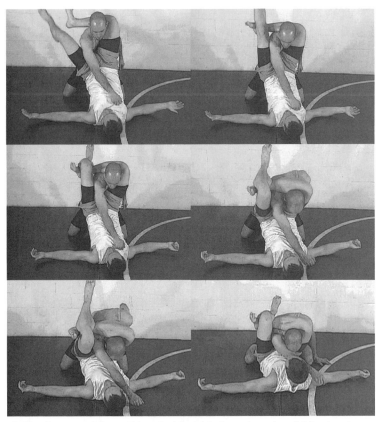

● Hook your short tail leg behind his head and pull him back quickly with this leg setting the figure-4 grip.
● Release and repeat on the other side.

Closed setup drill

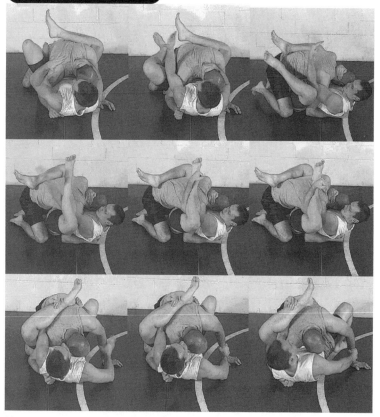

If you are able to maintain tight control with your opponent, then the following drill should serve you well.

● Overhook his right arm with your left arm.
● Underhook your left leg with your left arm.
● Attempt to gain a one-on-one wrist control of his left arm with your free hand.

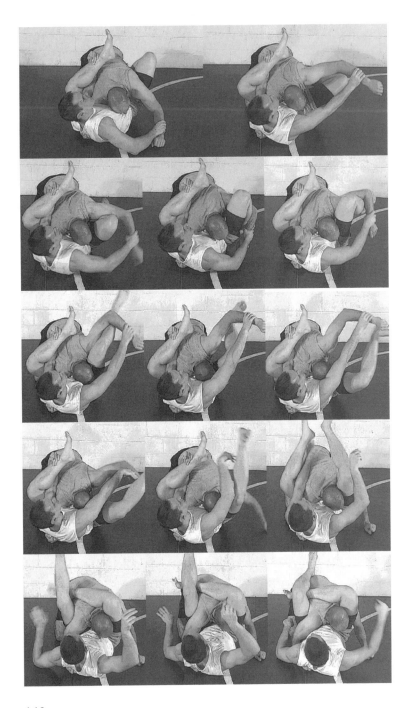

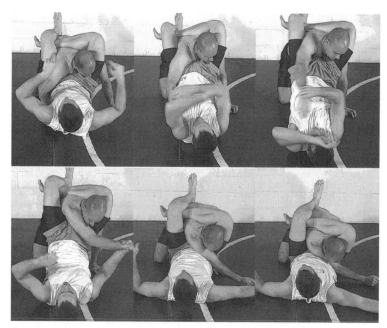

● As he fights out of it, allow his arm to travel to the outside.
● Insert your right knee under his right arm pit.
● Overhook his left arm with your right leg.
● Set your figure-4 grip and go to work.

Triangle follow drill

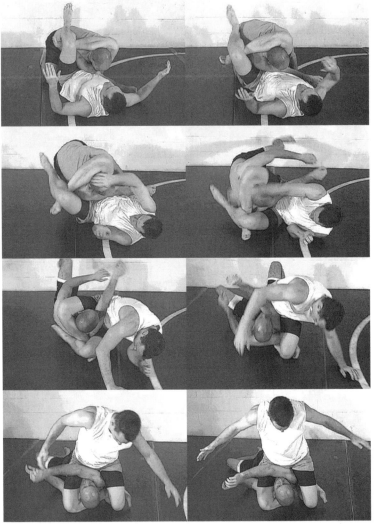

● Use the preceding drills to set.

● Once hooked, take it to the tap and then back off a comfortable inch or two and have your partner flop and/or roll through.

● Maintain the "slack" integrity of your triangle and strive to finish on your side and from the top saddle/mounted position.

Anti-slam

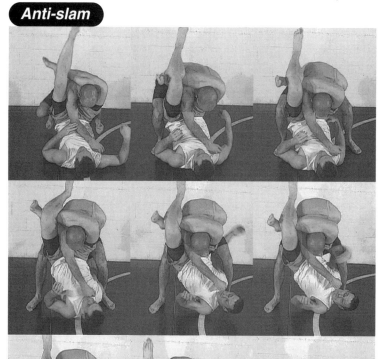

There have been more than a few memorable and vicious slams versus an attempted triangle. So it might be wise to drill for that contingency.

● Hook your partner with your triangle and back off to the comfortable zone.

● Allow him to attempt to lift you Quinton Jackson/Matt Hughes style.

● Underhook a supporting leg to keep yourself on terra firma.

● It is best to underhook the excluded leg, meaning if his right arm is included in the triangle, underhook his left leg and vice versa.

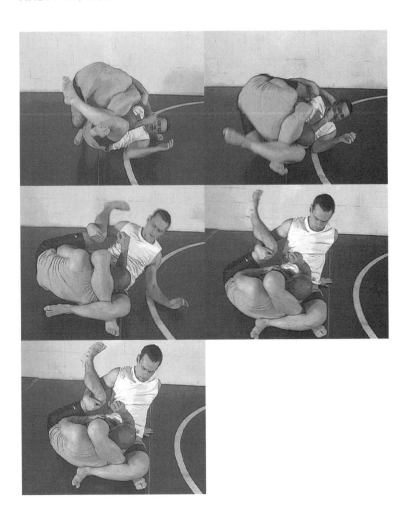

Triangle plus

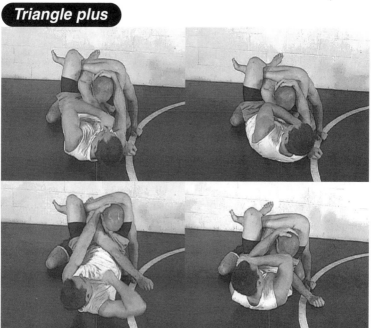

A nice bonus is that the triangle is practically the only bottom position that lends itself to ground and pound. Demian Maia rolled Ed Herman from a guard triangle to a mounted triangle and finished with strikes from there. Anderson Silva, in his match against Travis Lutter, let fly with elbows once he set his guard triangle. I suggest training and playing along that mind-set.

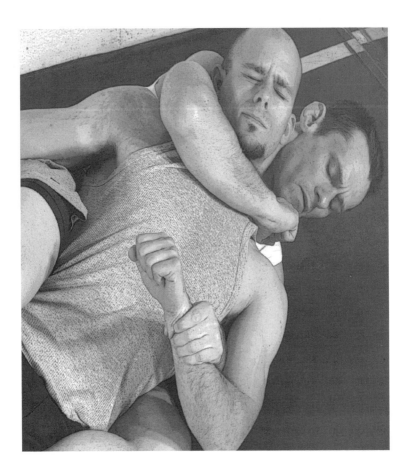

14 Shoulder choke / arm triangle

We've got seven victories with the shoulder choke/arm triangle, three in the UFC and four in Pride. Not a large number, but it does the job.

Shoulder choke / arm triangle

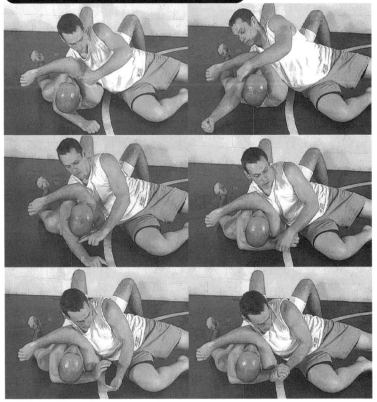

The form

The shoulder choke or arm triangle follows the standard triangle choke theory of three constricting surfaces — your opponent's own biceps and your biceps and forearm.

- Push his arm across his throat, here his right.
- Overhook his throat with your right arm.
- Encircle his head with your right arm.

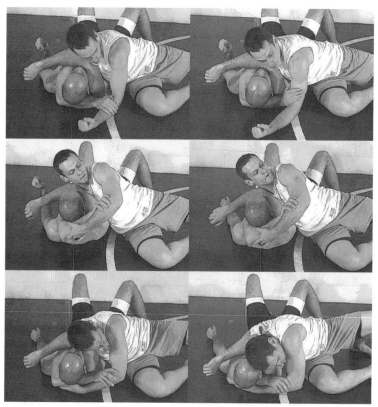

● Grip the forearm of the long tail arm (here your left). Yes, it usually hits with the biceps grip, but you'll find with a little experimentation, this is a much stronger grip.
● Drive your head into his while squeezing tightly.

Top saddle / mounted arm triangle

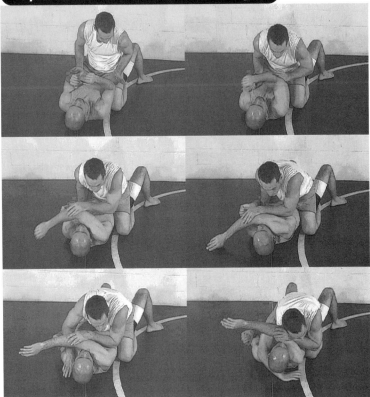

● Simply shove an arm over his throat. Your left palm will shove his right elbow and set the choke.

Hop to cross body

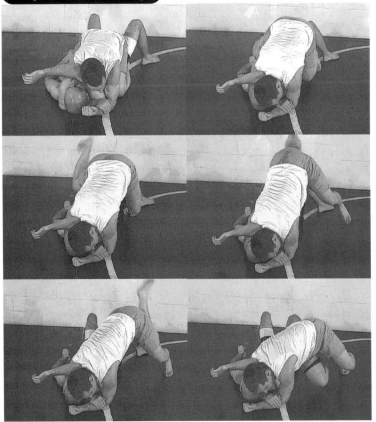

Once you have the mounted version set, you can often tighten your constricting surfaces by moving to cross body position.

● Set your mounted shoulder choke, here on his right side again.
● Hop off to his right side to tighten the compression.

Cross body to cross body arm triangle

Here's another nice transition used by Martin Kampmann versus Drew McFedries.

● Hit a cross body ride on your partner's left side.
● Underhook his far arm with your hip-side arm.
● Hop to the far side.
● Travel all the way across the body with the slide knee and finish the arm triangle on the far side.

1/2 guard / 1/2 mount arm triangle

Mario Sperry showed us just how possible this hook is.

● Inside the 1/2 guard, maneuver an arm across his throat, here his right, and hit the arm triangle.

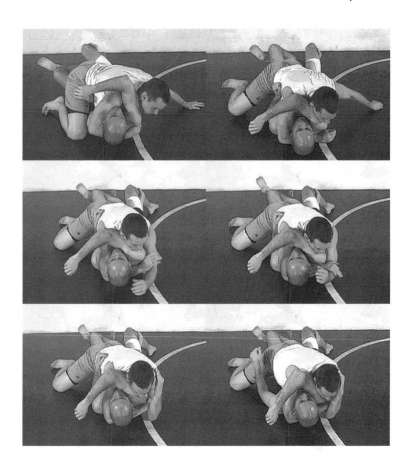

Hooks in ride to arm triangle

Eric Shafer used this beautiful transition in his match versus Rob MacDonald.

● Your partner is in the 1/4 position and you have hooks in.
● He rolls to his right.
● As he rolls, pop your hooks out.
● Keep his right arm trapped with the left side of your neck/head.
● Encircle his neck with your left arm.
● Hit the arm triangle.

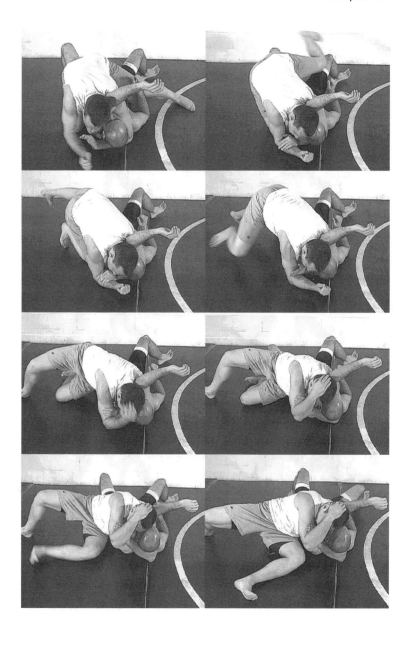

15 Heel hook

The heel hook contributed six total wins with five inside the Pride ring and only one in the UFC. Leg locks are highly regarded in grappling-only circles, and rightly so, but in straight MMA, we see much less success attacking the legs. To a large degree it seems some of the standard leg locking setups are not necessarily strike resistant, and that contributed to the poor showing of leg locks in general. I wager that smarter setups would up the success rate, but right now we'll concern ourselves with the leg lock that did make the grade.

Much of the heel hook's success is dependent on the grip, made all the more tenuous because the human foot is a slippery object to get a hold of. Not only are we grasping at an appendage hanging from the strongest limb on the body, but we are attempting to grip what is undoubtedly a slick-with-sweat portion of the human anatomy. The human foot can excrete up to a pint of sweat per day. Consider that when gripping at a sweaty, squirming athlete who is raring to hurt you.

I'd love to provide ingenious setups, but each heel hook seemed more a matter of luck than design since it fell into hands out of a scramble. In another volume we'll address revised leg-locking setups, combinations and transitions that translate to MMA. In this guide we'll satisfy ourselves with tightening that grip because without it no heel hook will work.

Heel hook

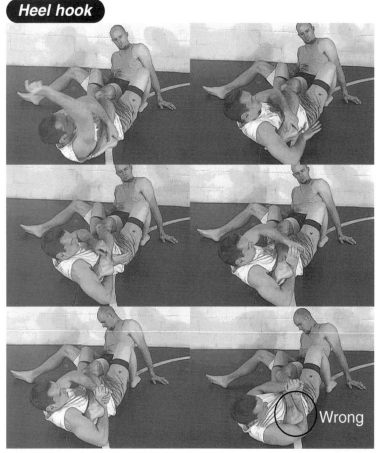

Wrong

The Grip

● Place the toes of the attacked foot underneath your attacking armpit.

● Underhook his heel with the attacking wrist — not the crook of the arm as the lever is too soft and more prone to slippage.

● Grip your hands in a palm-to-palm grip or reverse lever.

● Use whatever variety of leg ride you have managed (figure-4, scissors, shin wedge or jam) to stretch him.

● Torque his heel toward your centerline while arching your back, particularly on the armpit retention side, to place more stress on his ankle.

From top to bottom, stretching him out with a scissors, figure-4 and shin wedge.

Outliers and conclusion

In any statistical study you have what are known as outliers. These are results or phenomena that lie outside the mean or crest of the bell curve. What we have done with this volume is lay out a plan for working the tools of highest utility. By my arbitrary definition, I have designated any tool that contributed six or more wins as the cutoff point.

Of the 640 fights examined, there were 38 victories via outliers. Space considerations will not permit us to delve into the tools that provided 5 or fewer victories. That is a volume for a future day. In that volume we will explore these outliers and approach them like an engineer. We will demonstrate the outlier as it occurred and offer tightening tips that may allow a tool with low utility to move to a higher ranking.

In the meantime there is more than enough grist for the mill within this book. You've got a quantifiable way to examine what to include and what not to include in your training regimen. You've been introduced to fight metrics as it applies to MMA. And we've offered the highest percentage setups or execution tools for these top tools. In essence you have a guide book to the best of the best as demonstrated by the best athletes in the business. That's as solid a foundational plan as I can imagine.

Have fun, train hard, train safe and always keep those minds working!

Mark Hatmaker

Resources

BEST CHOICES

First, please visit my Web site at
www.extremeselfprotection.com
You will find even more training
material as well as updates and
other resources.

Amazon.com

The place to browse for books such
as this one and other similar titles.

Paladin Press
www.paladin-press.com

Paladin carries many training
resources as well as some of my
videos, which allow you to see
much of what is covered in my
NHB books.

Ringside Boxing
www.ringside.com

Best choice for primo equipment.

Sherdog.com

Best resource for MMA news, event
results and NHB happenings.

Threat Response Solutions
www.trsdirect.com

They also offer many training
resources along with some of my
products.

Tracks Publishing
www.startupsports.com

They publish all the books in the
NHBF series as well as a few fine
boxing titles.

www.humankinetics.com

Training and conditioning info.

www.matsmatsmats.com

Best resource for quality mats at
good prices.

Video instruction

Extreme Self-Protection
extremeselfprotection.com

Paladin Press
paladin-press.com

Threat Response Solutions
trsdirect.com

World Martial Arts
groundfighter.com

Events

IFC
ifc-usa.com

IVC
valetudo.com

King of the Cage
kingofthecage.com

Pancrase
so-net.ne.jp/pancrase

Pride
pridefc.com

The Ultimate Fighting
Championships
ufc.tv

Universal Combat Challenge
ucczone.ca/

Index

Index

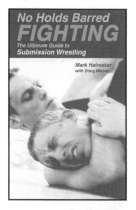

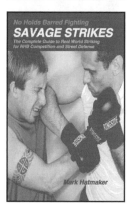

Boxing Mastery
Advance Techniques, Tactics and
Strategies from the Sweet Science
1-884654-21-5 / $12.95
Advanced boxing skills and ring general-
ship. 900 photos.

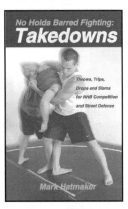

**No Holds Barred Fighting:
Takedowns**
Throws, Trips, Drops and Slams for NHB
Competition and Street Defense
1-884654-25-8 / $12.95
850 photos.

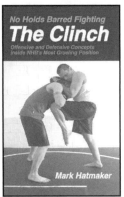

**No Holds Barred Fighting:
The Clinch**
Offensive and Defensive Concepts
Inside NHB's Most Grueling Position
1-884654-27-4 / $12.95
750 photos.

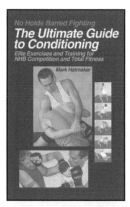

No Holds Barred Fighting:
The Ultimate Guide to Conditioning
Elite Exercises and Training for NHB
Competition and Total Fitness
1-884654-29-0 / $12.95
192 pages / 900 photos

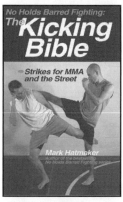

No Holds Barred Fighting:
The Kicking Bible
Strikes for MMA and the Street
1-884654-31-2 / $12.95
192 pages / 700 photos

No Second Chance:
A Reality-Based Guide to Self-Defense
How to avoid and survive an assault.
1-884654-32-0 / $12.95
500 photos.

Mark Hatmaker is the bestselling author of the *No Holds Barred Fighting Series, No Second Chance* and *Boxing Mastery*. He also has produced more than 40 instructional videos. His resume includes extensive experience in the combat arts including boxing, wrestling, Jiu-jitsu and Muay Thai.

He is a highly regarded coach of professional and amateur fighters, law enforcement officials and security personnel. Hatmaker founded Extreme Self Protection (ESP), a research body that compiles, analyzes and teaches the most effective Western combat methods known. ESP holds numerous seminars throughout the country each year including the prestigious Karate College/Martial Arts Universities in Radford, Virginia. He lives in Knoxville, Tennessee.